THE SEVEN WORDS OF JESUS FROM THE CROSS

MICHAEL L. FABER

ELK GROVE PUBLICATIONS

Second Edition Copyright 2016.
Michael L. Faber,
all rights reserved.

ISBN 13: 978-1-940781-15-0

Published by Elk Grove Publications

through Kindle Direct Publishing

You may reach brother Faber by e-mail at mfaber@elkgrove.net.

Elk Grove Publications

TABLE

THE SEVEN WORDS FROM THE CROSS CHRONOLOGICALY WITH SCRIPTURE REFERENCES

"Father, forgive them, for they do not know what they are doing." Luke 23:34

"I tell you the truth, today you will be with me in paradise." Luke 23:43

"Dear woman, here is your son" and to the disciple, "Here is your mother." John 19:26–27

"Eloi, Eloi, lama sabachthani?" –which means, "My God, my God, why have you forsaken me?" Matt. 27:46, Mark 15:34

"I am thirsty." John 19:28

"It is finished." John 19:30

"Father, into your hands I commit my spirit." Luke 23:46

INTRODUCTION

As we approach the Lenten season, Passion Week, and specifically Good Friday, it is common to reflect on the crucifixion of Jesus Christ. This is entirely appropriate. The crucifixion of Christ is very important to the plan of salvation. The Gospels of Matthew, Mark, Luke and John devote many pages of their text to the events leading up to and including the passion of Jesus Christ. These events start with the Triumphal entry into Jerusalem on Palm Sunday, and include his final teachings, the institution of the Lord's Supper, the washing of feet, the new Commandment, the betrayal by Judas, the fervent prayer of Jesus in the Garden of Gethsemane, His arrest, the denial by Peter, His trial before the Jewish Leaders, King Herod and Pilate, the angry mobs, finishing with His scourging and crucifixion. Far fewer pages of the gospels are devoted to the Resurrection.

The death of Jesus on the cross, held a great deal of attention in the early church. That is why Paul pronounced his famous words, "For I resolved to know nothing while I was with you except Jesus Christ and Him crucified." I Cor. 2:2. That is why we all use the Cross, in some manifestation, as a symbol of our faith. It is quite popular, during this time of reflection on the crucifixion of Jesus, to ponder on the words He spoke from the cross. Panning through the four Gospels, we find seven sayings from Jesus which He proclaimed during His crucifixion. Only one of these sayings is repeated in two different Gospels. The other six are mentioned only in one Gospel.

I have made a table of all seven sayings with Scripture references. In the following two chapters, we will deal with all seven sayings. The first chapter deals with the sayings which reveal how Jesus suffered for us, focusing on the only saying which was repeated in Gospels twice: "My God, my God, why have you forsaken me?" The second chapter focuses on those saying by Jesus which prove that even while He was suffering and dying for us, He was still caring for those around Him. I hope the thoughts and words in this little booklet are a blessing to you. May they bring you closer to our Lord and Savior, Jesus Christ.

The Seven Words of Jesus from the Cross

CHAPTER ONE

THERE IS NO RESURRECTION WITHOUT A CRUCIFIXION

At my home, I have a beautiful carved wooden crucifix which I imported from Vietnam. It hangs over my bed. One day, one of my Pentecostal friends came visiting. He looked at the crucifix and declared, "Jesus rose from that tomb in victory over death!" and as quickly as the words were out of his mouth, I replied, "Yes, and He also died on that cross for the forgiveness of your sins!"

Sometimes we are in such a hurry to get to Easter, we rush right past Good Friday. But while everyone likes a happy ending, a story is not interesting without conflict and pain. So it is with the Gospel story of Jesus Christ. While much can be discussed about the meaning of the resurrection of Christ, surely there can be no resurrection without a crucifixion.

We are told in the Gospels how Jesus was captured by the Jewish leadership and turned over to the Roman authorities. We walk with Jesus as He was tried by Governor Pilate, scourged, beaten ridiculed, stripped of the clothing and brutally nailed to a cross. Then as He hung there, a man, who only a few days earlier had been hailed by the crowds as the long awaited Messiah and the King of the Jews, was mocked by these crowds and even by the criminals with whom He was dying. We are told by Matthew and Mark how, in a moment of despair, He cries out in a loud voice using archaic words of his native language, *"Eloi, Eloi, lama sabachthani!"* These Aramaic or Hebrew words were quoted from Psalm 22, meaning "MY GOD, MY GOD, WHY HAVE YOU FORSAKEN ME?"

If Jesus were God, how could He utter these words? Is it possible for God to forsake Himself? Didn't He know all along that it was the Father's plan for Him to die? Didn't He even state at the Last Supper "...Take and eat; this is my body," and "...Drink from it all of you. This is my blood of the covenant, which is poured out for many for the forgiveness of sins"? Matt. 26:26–28. Of course, Jesus knew all along that His purpose was to die on the cross.

If you know the story, this was the culmination of God's plan since mankind fell to sin in the Garden of Eden. God had created man for fellowship with Him, but Satan took the form of a serpent to trick Eve and then Adam to disobey God. Sin broke the bond of fellowship between God and man, and required punishment, because God is just. Because of this act of rebellion, mankind was cursed with the plague of sin and death and could not enjoy eternal fellowship with God as He desired. From time eternal, it was known that "without the shedding of blood there is no forgiveness." Heb. 9:22b.

The Old Covenant was established between God and His chosen people, the Jews, to establish a sacrificial system where blood of an innocent lamb or goat would be spilt for the forgiveness of particular acts of sin. But this system was imperfect and temporary. For the blood of bulls and goats could not take away sins. cf Heb. 10:4. But by one sacrifice, Jesus was able to "make perfect forever those who are being made holy. Heb. 10:14. The only thing innocent enough, and worthy enough to constitute an *adequate* sacrifice for all sin for all time, would be God Himself. Through Christ, we may be reconciled with God, if we will perservere by doing the will of God. Heb. 10:36.

For this reason, "The Word became flesh and made his dwelling among us." John 1:14. God the Son, "Who being in very nature God…made himself nothing, …being made in human likeness. And being found in appearance as a man, he humbled himself and became obedient to death—even death on a cross!" Php. 2:6–8. In other words, God the Son who was all powerful in the celestial heights consented to lower himself to take on the body of a man to allow Himself, as someone entirely worthy and entirely innocent, to be made the sacrifice for all of our sins! He allowed His blood to be spilt for the forgiveness of sin, so that all of us all could be reconciled to the Father. This was the plan all along. The Incarnation, the life, the death... Jesus knew "it was for this reason" that he came. He predicted quite clearly while still in Galilee "The Son of Man is going to be delivered into the hands of men. They will kill him, and on the third day he will be raised to life." Matt. 17:22–23.

If all this is true, then why the seeming second thoughts by Jesus at His hour of trial? We can understand this in several ways. First, Jesus was proclaiming a fulfillment of prophecy, and second, He was demonstrating something wonderful about the sacrifice He was making, which can only be understood by understanding the Nature of Christ, Himself.

FULFILLMENT OF PSALM 22

While Psalm 22 was originally written as an individual lament, the writers of the Gospel saw the Holy Spirit at work predicting the Passion of Christ. It is uncanny how many similarities there are between the details of this Psalm and the crucifixion of Christ. While the writer of this Psalm undoubtedly thought that he was writing about his own troubles, in all likelihood, the Holy Spirit was at work helping him pen what would become one of the most beloved messianic psalms.

Psalm 22:1 begins with these very words, "My God, my God, why have you forsaken me? Why are you so far from saving me, so far from my cries of anguish?" Undoubtedly, Jesus felt the same way. He had always felt a great closeness to the Father, but now everything was crashing around Him. Writers on this topic opine that as He took the sin of the world upon Himself, in accordance with the Divine Plan, the Father was forced to look away, even if for a second, and it is at this time, that the Son felt a great emptiness and abandonment which He had never before experienced.

In the Psalm, enemies cried out, "He trusts in the Lord. Let the Lord rescue him!" Psalm 22:8. Matthew records that they taunted Jesus with the same words as He hung on the cross. cf Matt. 27:43. Of course these were words of temptation, just like the devil's taunts to Jesus in the desert, "If you are the Son of God, throw yourself down." Matt. 4:6a. They were meant to cause Jesus to question His role and His relationship. They added spiritual and emotional pressure to His physical pain.

In the Psalm it states, "...and my tongue sticks to the roof of my mouth." Psalm 22:15. At the crucifixion, Jesus declared, "I AM THIRSTY." John 19:28. Despite some of the heresies circulating in early Christianity that Jesus' divinity prevented him from suffering, or only made him *appear* as man, the truth is, that He suffered mightily on that cross. He felt hunger. He felt thirst. He felt pain.

In the Psalm it declares, "They pierce my hands and my feet." Psalm 22:16b. We know that as they prepared to lift Him up, they drove nails through His hands and feet to attach him to the Cross.

Finally, the Psalmist complains, "They divide my clothes among them and cast lots for my garments." Psalm 22:18. This is exactly what the Roman guards did at the foot of the cross, while Jesus was hanging there. cf Matt. 27:35.

Surely, these similarities were not lost on Jesus as He hung there. Perhaps He declared these famous words as a shorthand for saying, "See guys, this is happening just as predicted by the Psalmist hundreds of years ago! The prophecies are fulfilled. I am really am the Messiah!"

Other writers have pointed out, that while the original Psalm begins with the lonely cries of the Psalmist in the midst of his rejection, suffering, and abandonment, the Psalm ends with a cry of faith and victory. "Posterity will serve him; future generations will be told about the Lord. They will proclaim his righteousness declaring to a people yet unborn: *He has done it*!" Psalm 22:30–31.

Indeed, because of Christ's faithfulness on the cross, "we have been made holy through the sacrifice of the body of Jesus Christ once for all." Hebrews 10:10. By His sacrifice, He preserved a place for future generations and they have proclaimed *HIS* righteousness in place of their own. Indeed, He accomplished it! That is why in His final words from the cross, He would declare "IT IS FINISHED." John 19:30.

Of course we are taught that God's work in us is a work in progress. While Jesus did all the heavy lifting on the cross at one point in time, He still is in the process of perfecting us as we become holy. It is an interesting side note that the Greek word for "It is finished" is tetelestai which is in the Greek grammatical perfect tense. What this means is that the verb "finish" is something that happened in the past, but the effects of which are still being felt by us today. Jesus finished paying the price on the cross, once in history, but we still feel the effects of His saving work as we are being sanctified by the Holy Spirit, and as His body and blood are being re-presented to us in the Mass. He is not re-sacrificed, but we are able to experience the effects freshly as we participate in his body and blood. cf 1 Cor 10:16.

CHRIST AS FULLY GOD AND FULLY MAN

We should not be lulled by the above analysis of Psalm 22 into thinking that Jesus was not truly suffering physically, emotionally and even spiritually as he uttered the words, "My God, my God, why have you forsaken me?" These words actually reveal God's love for us in the greatest way possible.

Early Christians struggled to understand the nature of Christ. They knew that He was God. "For in Christ all the fullness of the Deity lives in bodily form." Col. 2:9. But could God suffer or be hurt by mere nails and spears? Early heretics declared that Jesus only *appeared* to suffer.

But early Christians also understood that Jesus was really a man, not just a ghost or an appearance. For He was like us "in every way, in order that he might become a *merciful* and faithful high priest in service to God, and that he might make atonement for the sins of the people. Because he himself suffered when he was tempted, he is able to help those who are being tempted." Heb. 2:17–18. In other words, He is fully God, thus His sacrifice was of sufficient worth to cover the sins of all mankind, but He was also fully man in order to make the sacrifice fair. Man (Jesus) paid the price for the sin of man(kind). Furthermore, now that God, through the Son, has joined fully with Man, He can truly understand and truly feel the temptations and the pain we suffer, so that He could be even *more merciful and more understanding* if that is even possible.

Stated another way, Jesus was fully man, so that His sacrifice would not be a *cheap* sacrifice. It would be nothing if God just sent a hologram or a divine form incapable of being tempted or feeling pain, just to put on a show. No. His innocence from sin was genuine because He was truly tempted and had to struggle to overcome temptation just as we do. His sacrifice truly cost HIM something because He truly felt pain and anguish just as we do.

Christians later understood that Jesus is fully God and fully man. What does this mean? As a real man, Jesus had feelings and emotions just like the rest of us. He had an instinct to survive just like the rest of us. Yes. He knew the divine plan for Him to die, yet deep in His human heart, He harbored the hope that somehow the Father would come through and spare Him. He had known the praise and adulation and love of the people as they proclaimed him Messiah and King just a few days before. Now, He felt their rejection and scorn. Even at the Garden of Gethsemane, His human nature, and His desire to survive was apparent, as the prayed the words, "My Father, if it is possible, may this cup be taken from me." Matt. 26:39. He was hoping against hope that the Father would somehow spare him. Now hanging on the cross, He realized that this hope was in vain. He knew the plan spiritually and intellectually, but emotionally, He could not help but cry out, "My God, my God, why have you forsaken me?"

Why is this wonderful news? It means that God, through the Son, now understands exactly what we are going through in our moments of weakness. He can't blame us because He was there and He knows how we feel. It means that it is possible to overcome temptation and weakness just as Jesus did, because he was tempted in every way, and He still overcame. It means that God loves you and me so much that He lowered Himself from the joy and bliss of pure divinity to unite with the weakness of human flesh to experience loneliness, grief, humiliation, pain, and death, yes…even death on a cross, so that we can be united with Him in divinity and enjoy eternal life, if only we will place our faith in Him. From the cross, at His moment of physical death, Jesus knew that it was not over. "FATHER, INTO YOUR HANDS I COMMIT MY SPIRIT." He declared. Luke 23:46. While His body was dying He knew His Spirit would be reunited with the Father in His loving embrace, and soon to be re-united with His resurrected body.

When we believe in Christ, we can also have confidence that our spirits and eventually our resurrected bodies reunited with our spirit will live on in God's loving embrace. "For God so loved the world, that He gave His only begotten Son, so that whosoever believes in Him, shall not perish but have everlasting life." John 3:16. God loves you, my friend. He wants to have you as His friend and His companion for all eternity. He wants this so much that He became one of us to die a terrible death to pay the price for our sin, so that we can be united with Him in Faith.

On the cross, He called out, "MY GOD, MY GOD, WHY HAVE YOU FORSAKEN ME?" But the Father did NOT forsake Him. He raised Jesus from the dead on the third day, just as it had always been planned. By dying, He conquered sin, by rising, He destroyed the power of death. Now He calls out to you… "Come unto me."

The question, my friends, is "How will we respond to this holy invitation?" Jesus showed His love for us by dying in our place. Knowing the extent of His sacrifice, knowing the pain He felt on that cross, will we respond in love, by living for Him?

He died to pay the price for our sin. We will repay Him by continuing to live in it? Or understanding what Jesus did, will we instead repent of our sins and confess them, relying on God's promise of forgiveness?

CHAPTER TWO

JESUS WAS BUSY: EVEN ON THE CROSS

In the last chapter, we delved into four of the seven sentences Jesus spoke from the cross, as we meditated on the fact that *There is no Resurrection without a Crucifixion*. As we thought about the suffering of Jesus on the cross, we looked at His words, "MY GOD, MY GOD, WHY HAVE YOU FORSAKEN ME?" also "I AM THIRSTY", as well as "FATHER, INTO YOUR HANDS I COMMIT MY SPIRIT" and finally, "IT IS FINISHED."

All of these words spoke of the suffering and death of Christ, but now we will look at what else He said, and realize that even as He was dying for us, He was taking care of the business of ministry. One of the marks of Jesus' ministry is that He was always thinking of others. Of course, this is why He came to earth in the first place. He loved mankind so much, He wanted to redeem us for an everlasting relationship with the Father. Having made the decision to lower himself to unite with human flesh, He spent His days and nights here, caring and providing for His lost sheep.

One of the most poignant scenes that comes to mind is what happened immediately after hearing that his beloved cousin, John the Baptist, had been brutally murdered by King Herod. As we mentioned before, Jesus was fully man as well as fully God, and He was just as subject to weariness and distress as we are. He was distraught over the death of His loved one and wanted to withdraw to a lonely place to have some time by Himself. You or I would want the same. After a heavy schedule of public ministry and a severe personal loss, of course we would want, even need, some time by ourselves. The crowd was not so understanding and continued to follow him along the shore.

When evening came and Jesus could see that they were hungry, He had compassion on them. He could have said, "Can't you see I need some alone time? Go home!" In fact, His disciples urged Him to do just that. But instead, He declared, "They do not need to go away. You give them something to eat." Matt. 14:16. Then He proceeded to perform the greatest miracle of His ministry by feeding the 5000. You see, that is how Jesus was. He was always thinking of others. As we will see by looking at the remaining words Jesus spoke from the cross, He was busy thinking of others as He spoke words of Forgiveness, Provision and Promise.

FORGIVENESS

Jesus did not change His personality, or His character, even as they were nailing His hands and His feet to that wooden cross. One of the first words He uttered, even as the Roman soldiers were in the process of killing Him was "FATHER, FORGIVE THEM, FOR THEY DO NOT KNOW WHAT THEY ARE DOING."

Luke 23:34.

Forgiveness is what Jesus came to the earth to accomplish. "Through Jesus the forgiveness of sins is proclaimed to you." Acts 13:38. According to John, "your sins have been forgiven on account of his name." I John 2:12. "We have been made holy through the sacrifice of the body of Jesus Christ once for all." Hebrews 10:10. Not only did Jesus come to accomplish forgiveness on our behalf, He also commanded us as His followers to forgive if we want to be forgiven. cf Matt.6:14–15. This was a major point of his earthly ministry and even included in the Lord's Prayer. Over and over, Jesus hammered home the point in His teachings that we need to forgive our brothers and sisters, just as we want our Father in heaven to forgive us. It is no surprise then that Jesus would carry on the work of forgiveness, even as He was dying on the cross.

Can you imagine being in Jesus' situation? You have been betrayed by your friends and your people, and the leaders of the religion which supposedly worships you (remember Jesus was also fully God). They have handed you over to enemies and demanded your death. Then, your enemies have mocked you, scourged you, marched you through the streets, and are now hammering spikes into your hands and feet! What pain! What humiliation! You could call death down on these infidels who are hurting and abusing you, but what do you do instead? "Father, forgive them, for they know not what they do." You utter words of forgiveness and restoration.

Do we ever think about what it meant to be the young man who was ordered to hammer those nails? Was he sadistic, enjoying this infliction of pain on an innocent man? If so, what caused him to become this way? Was he fearful, having heard that this Jew was a holy man, reputed to be able to perform great miracles? Did he worry that Jesus would utter a curse on him, or call down death? Did he even know who Jesus was? Did he feel guilty and remorseful for having to carry out this cruel act? Had his heart been hardened to the pain of others after performing this task many times before? We don't know. But surely this young man was as much a victim of this cruel and heartless system as Jesus was. Jesus saw beyond the armor and the spear, and the helmet of Rome. He saw the heart of a young man who was once an innocent boy. This young man was loved by the Father and still caught up in a cruel world system of sin and oppression. It was for this young man that Jesus came to die.

No, He did not call down curses or death. He commenced to fulfilling His mission by speaking words of life to this young man. He spoke words of forgiveness, which opened the door for a possibility of repentance. We do not know what happened to this young man, and the others present there that day, but I like to think that they reflected on the death and resurrection of Christ and remembered these words of forgiveness, thus receiving eternal life. Perhaps, as new believers, they were among those who received Paul's epistle to the Romans.

PROVISION

While Jesus was dying on the cross, He wasn't just thinking of Himself, but He was still concerned about the welfare of others. He had instituted the Kingdom of God, and His subjects needed to be cared for; not just spiritually, but physically. Jesus had been caring for the whole person during His entire ministry. He didn't just preach at people and tell them to repent and say a prayer, but He also cared for them emotionally by comforting and loving them, and He cared for them physically by curing their diseases and feeding them when they were hungry.

Lest we forget, Jesus had a mother. Mary was about 14 or 15 years old when she bore the Christ child, so if He was now dying at age 33, that meant she would be about 48. Since Joseph is never mentioned anywhere in Scripture after the incident when Jesus was 12, scholars assume Joseph had passed away and Mary was dependent upon her son, Jesus, for support. Now, in fulfillment of His heavenly mission, He was dying. What was to become of Mary? Who would take care of her? She had been faithful to God to carry the Christ child under socially unacceptable conditions. God would not abandon her. As Jesus hung there on the cross, Jesus looked down and saw His mother there standing next to young John, "the disciple that Jesus loved." cf John 19:26. He said to his mother,

"Woman, here is your son," and to the disciple, "Here is your mother." Scripture then records that from that time on, this disciple took her into his home. cf John 19:26b–27.

In essence, Jesus made a last will and testament from the cross. He chose, John, His youngest disciple, to take care of His mother for the rest of her days on earth until she was reunited with her son in heaven. John faithfully carried out this mission.

As an aside, one might wonder why Jesus gave his mother to the care of His disciple John when scripture records that He had brothers and sisters. The Church has always believed that Mary was a virgin, not just before the birth of Jesus, but during her whole life. The "brothers and sisters" spoken of in the gospels were actually cousins or more distant relatives. In modern language we might use the terms "relatives" rather than brothers or sisters. If the Church's understanding of Mary's perpetual virginity was incorrect, and if in fact she had other children after Jesus, they would have the duty to take care of their mother by law and by custom, and what Jesus did from the cross would make no sense. On the other hand, if Mary had no children other than Jesus, then His provision for her by putting her into the able care of John makes perfect sense.

Jesus was busy on the cross. Not just dying, not just supplying forgiveness for the sins of all mankind and for individual Roman guards, but also making sure that the physical needs of his mother would be provided for. We, too, also need to make sure we are providing for the physical and emotional needs of our loved ones as we busy ourselves with our spiritual and earthly tasks.

PROMISE

While Jesus was busy dying on the cross, not only was he taunted by the Roman Guards and the crowd, but even his fellow convicts. Three of the four Gospels record that Jesus was crucified between two robbers or criminals. While the Son of God normally occupied a place in the Trinity between the Father and the Holy Spirit, now in the midst of His great sacrifice, he shared company with two criminals condemned to death.

Luke records the conversation between these men. The first criminal mimicked the taunts of the crowds and the guards, stating, "Aren't you the Messiah? Save yourself and us!" Luke 23:39b It is amazing how even in the midst of so much death and pain, we humans can attempt to make ourselves feel better by putting others down. Here this man was, at the bottom of society, half naked and nailed to a piece of wood, and still he sought to elevate himself socially by taunting another.

The other criminal saw exactly what was happening and he rebuked the first with the words, "Don't you fear God, since you are under the same sentence? We are punished justly, for we are getting what our deeds deserve. But this man has done nothing wrong." Luke 23:40–41. Once He had duly rebuked his fellow criminal, the second man then uttered a very primitive statement of faith. "Jesus, remember me when you come into your kingdom." Luke 23:42. Notice he didn't declare Jesus was God, or articulate the nature of the trinity, or even ask Jesus to raise him from the dead. He did believe that Jesus was the King of some future kingdom and perhaps might be able to reward him for his declaration of loyalty. "Remember me" was the only request. But Jesus took this kernel of faith and grew it into a wonderful corn stock bearing eternal fruit when He replied, "I TELL YOU THE TRUTH, TODAY YOU WILL BE WITH ME IN PARADISE." Luke 23:43.

The robber asked to be remembered, and Jesus gave him eternal life. John quoted Jesus earlier in his ministry when He was speaking to Nicodemus, "For God so loved the world, that He gave His only begotten Son, that whosoever believes in Him shall not perish but have everlasting life." John 3:16. The thief had placed his hope in Jesus and Jesus did not disappoint. The life of this thief was over. It had run its course, and come to no good end. All the thief had to look forward to was several more hours of suffering and humiliation, then inevitable death. But Jesus changed all that in one instant. Perhaps there was a future for this sorry man after all.

What had been hopeless was now

filled with hope. What had been sad was now joyous! He had a future now, and it lay with his King, Jesus Christ. "I tell you the truth, today you will be with me in paradise." It is true that day, Jesus was dying on the cross, but he was busy giving hope to the hopeless and telling the dying man that, indeed, there was a great promise for him.

Brothers and sisters, that same promise is for us if we will only place our trust in Jesus Christ. Will we believe in Jesus, the only begotten son of God? Will we place our hope in Him? He will not disappoint. In his epistle to the Romans, Paul declares, "if you confess with your mouth, 'Jesus is Lord' and believe in your heart that God raised him from the dead, you will be saved. For it is with your heart that you believe and are justified, and it is with your mouth that you profess your faith and are saved. As the Scripture says, 'Anyone who trusts in him will never be put to shame.'" Romans 10:9–11.

On that dark day, the thief put his trust in Jesus. It is amazing when you think of it. Here was Jesus dying right beside him. He was not getting off the cross as everyone told him to do. His life was seemingly coming to an end as well, and yet the thief still believed.

Sometimes, Jesus seems hard to believe. We want to throw Him away in the face of seeming science or seeming logic, or societal trends. Perhaps believing in Jesus is uncool or counter cultural. Hanging on the cross, He does not seem that powerful, or much like a King at all, and yet the thief still believed. There was something about Jesus that was compelling. His words rang true. His actions were notable.

"I am the resurrection and the life. He who believes in me will live, even though he dies; and whoever lives and believes in me will never die. Do you believe this?" John 11:25–26. The thief believed, and Jesus returned that trust with a promise, "I tell you the truth, today you will be with me in paradise." That day the thief was brought into paradise. That promise is for you and me as well.

REFLECTION

If you would like to take advantage of Jesus' Forgiveness, His Provision, and His Promise, you start with simple faith. Jesus can save instantly, as He did the thief on the cross, but usually, He has a life time of discipleship and spiritual growth planned for us. Faith begins as a gift from God which we must decide to first receive and then act upon. We must decide to receive this gift, and then we must respond in love by offering our lives in return as disciples of the Master. We join the Church that Jesus founded and receive the gifts of baptism for the forgiveness of sin and confirmation and holy communion to help us in our daily walk. We will also take advantage of other gifts that Christ offers us through the other sacraments. We decide to follow Him by learning more of His words and commands by reading and studying the Bible. We respond in love to Christ by offering our lives in holiness and service. We can communicate daily with Jesus through prayer.

As we grow in Christ, let us look to His example on the cross. Like Christ, let us constantly think of others first, even when we ourselves might find ourselves in extreme circumstances.

APPENDIX: JESUS DIDN'T STAY THERE

While the crucifixion and death of Christ are extremely important to our understanding of God's plan of salvation for us, we do not leave Christ on the cross forever, nor do we leave Him buried in the tomb. While it is entirely appropriate to meditate on the cost Jesus paid for us and His ultimate sacrifice which made our salvation possible, we should also remember the words of the angels to the women who came to anoint the body of our fallen Lord. "Why do you look for the living among the dead? He is not here; he has risen!" Luke 24:5–6.

Jesus died to pay the price for our sins, and He rose again to conquer death. All of us who were baptized into Christ Jesus were baptized into His death. cf

Romans 6:3. Paul declares, "We were therefore buried with him through baptism into death in order that, just as Christ was raised from the dead through the glory of the Father, we too may live a new life." Romans 6:4.

Yes, Jesus is the Crucified Christ, but He is also the Risen Lord. He died that we may be reconciled to the Father, and He rose again so that we may live forever with Him! This is the glorious message of Easter Sunday. Our crucified Lord has risen! He is risen indeed!

ABOUT THE AUTHOR

Michael Faber has been a bi–vocational preacher of the Gospel and California lawyer. He has been preaching since 1993 at various churches in Northern California. Brother Faber graduated from Fuller Seminary in 2012 with a Masters Degree in Theology and Bible. He is bilingual in English and Vietnamese, and also speaks some Chinese Mandarin, German, Greek, and Hebrew. He has ministered in the Sacramento, California area to senior citizens and several Vietnamese–American churches. He recently converted to Catholicism. His sermons have been recorded and shared in the U.S. and in Vietnam through www.vietchristian.com. In 2013 he published his first devotional book *Meditations on the Lord's Prayer* and in 2014 published *Keys to a Happy Life:*

The Beatitudes According to Jesus. Both books were published in United States and India. *Meditations on the Lord's Prayer* was also published in Vietnam. His sermons have been published in English, Vietnamese, Telugu, Tamil, and Hindi. You may reach Brother Faber by e–mail at mfaber@elkgrove.net.

www.ingramcontent.com/pod-product-compliance
Lightning Source LLC
Chambersburg PA
CBHW021454080526
44588CB00009B/839